Never Modern

Irénée Scalbert and 6a architects

⊓ PARK BOOKS

6a, the name, is a coincidence. The practice was born out of circumstances, at a particular time – 1998 – in a particular place – 6a, Orde Hall Street, London. Four architects met to participate in a design competition.[1] Their project needed to be entered under a name. Someone suggested '6a' and the name stayed.

The name does not indicate a polemic, like 'OMA'. It does not designate a signature, like 'Herzog & de Meuron'. It does not presume an attitude, like '9H' (the hardest pencil lead available). It is anonymous and it makes no presumption about personality, project or method.

In 6a's own words, 'we can be a bit more flexible and nimble about who, how and what.' Likewise the body of work completed by 6a to-date does not advertise an explicit theoretical position and it has not coalesced into a recognisable style. To the contrary, 6a are by their own admission 'reasonably promiscuous' in their choice of sources and influences, and catholic in their tastes. In the end, as they put it, 'it's all work.'

This essay takes stock of conversations that I had with them over a period of years, conversations that have often lasted into the early hours of the morning. It outlines elements for a theory of architecture but it is in the nature of conversations to fall short of a theory, a fact that suits 6a's temperament as well as my own. In the last two years, the word 'bricolage' has featured somewhat insistently. It is surely relevant to the work of 6a. And it provides me, if not with a method for what follows, then with a holdall for ideas prompted by our conversations.

Bricolage not withstanding, 6a's two partners followed what appears, in hindsight, an unusually coherent trajectory. Tom Emerson began his studies in the shadow of Peter Smithson at the University of Bath.

He and Stephanie Macdonald studied with Tony Fretton who, with his customary generosity to younger peers, taught them at the Royal College of Art for no fee or salary. There they met with Richard Wentworth and they became friends. Macdonald then took her Diploma with Adam Caruso and Peter St John at London Metropolitan University. The Smithsons were mastheads for the architects sometimes labelled as the Whisperers.[2]

The Whisperers had as their mentor Tony Fretton. Tony Fretton passed onto Peter St John his first commission. Peter St John and Adam Caruso collaborated with Wentworth on the Walsall Art Gallery. And so on.

In this episode of British architecture, the Smithsons and Wentworth stand like bookends, like the forward and the postscript to a long-drawn conversation on ordinariness, the everyday and their aesthetic possibilities.

It is the fate of architecture movements to find their fulfilment and their conclusion in forms, and it falls upon younger architects to inject new life into older forms. 6a is such a practice. They are clearly indebted to their forebears.

Witness for instance the alignment, at the rear of the gallery at Raven Row, of the window sill with the street pavement, first tried by Fretton in the Lisson Gallery.

Witness, too, the garden room at the South London Gallery, reminiscent of the café (or what used to be one) on the terrace of the Walsall Art Gallery designed by Caruso St John: both are clad with feather-like slates of two colours, both are punctured with windows that register the revolution of the sun and the time of the day.

But 6a speak a different language. They do not feel a moral imperative to articulate an intellectual position. They do not lay claim to being artists. Their charisma is directed outwards and it manifests itself first and foremost in their curiosity.

Situation

'The subject is what surrounds you.' The comment was made by 6a about Wentworth.[3] But it applies equally to 6a. Architects may not choose the subject to which they, like artists, give expression, but they are no less immersed in their task, surrounded by and within reach of the things that matter to them – site, materials, tools and participants. When 6a extended and refurbished an 18th-century house in Spitalfields, London, into an art gallery, now known as Raven Row, they had to come to terms with the fact that, for the most part, the life history of the building was invisible.

It could be glimpsed in a few archive photographs. Occasionally, with the right degree of attention, it could be detected in a detail of the fabric.

But the more familiar the architects became with the fabric, the less it seemed to be that of an 18th century building. Rather it was an 18th century canvas that provided support for narratives, some old and faint, some new and of the architects' own making. 6a often refer to narratives, every sign or detail in a fabric being an invitation to pull the thread of a story and to weave it into a local history. Raven Row is a listed building and it demanded this degree of attention. But the story-telling aspect of history is natural to 6a for whom the fastidious, convoluted stories of Georges Perec have long been references. 6a are at home, even at play among the debris of the past, and they ascribe to lives and places a common process of change.

In the 1980s, there still existed, at 41 Artillery Lane (a few doors away from Raven Row), a grocer, newsagent and tobacconist by the name of Samuel Stores. The building had been in the same hands since 1912, until it was bought and 'saved' by the Spitalfields Trust. All traces of occupancy were scraped down to the bare canvas until, as the historian Raphael Samuel recalls, all that was left was 'that fantasy object, 'an elegant merchant's house'.[4] The building had been socially and aesthetically upgraded until what had begun as a modest weaver's house had become 'a showcase of the restorer's arts.'

Attempts at returning buildings to their original condition, Samuel claimed, robs them of the very quality for which they are prized, oldness, leaving behind shells that show no sign of wear and tear and are innocent of history. If conservation is to have a meaning, it must take into account the complete life-cycle of a building, every mark being in principle worth preserving. 6a are not in the main motivated by the conservation of the past and they differ in this sense from historians. But they retain an appetite for the lost, unexpected detail, for what was discarded or forgotten in the course of time. 6a work like detectives. They are hungry for clues. They delight in the archive, in the chance find – such as their discovery of archival photographs of 56 Artillery Lane at the London Metropolitan Archive.

One of their favourite pictures in the set, dated 1972, shows the corner of a bed, a radio, the wallpaper and the glow of a window, affording an unexpected glimpse of a life that has since become invisible. An image may have a strong aesthetic appeal but ultimately it is valued as a hypothesis, as a sign of something past.

Another picture of a classical doorway devastated by fire at Raven Row may be 'an incredibly beautiful image', so compelling as to prompt experiments in cladding with charred timber. But its value lies as much in its surprising tectonic quality as in its being an enigma, a brief but violent aperçu of the past.

Other architects have demonstrated a keen sensibility towards the past, for instance Tony Fretton for the cumulation of the everyday and Caruso St John for tradition and its continuity. But what distinguishes 6a's sensibility is less a sense of the virtuous than a forensic curiosity, a frame of mind that is specifically historical. Architecture involves some detective work. You look at things, you look under and through things because they are a source of knowledge, signs of a momentary resourcefulness.

You then set yourself objectives and find the means to attain them. A picture suggests building in charcoal, then you experiment, you play with fire (literally in the case of Raven Row).

Intervention

A difficulty facing the architect is how to negotiate a past that concerns the detective and the historian and a future that is of interest to the client and the occupants. At Raven Row, the task on the one hand was to manage a slightly broken history – the exacting demands imposed by the conservation of a grade I-listed building, and the desire to maintain and enhance the significance of its fabric. On the other, it entailed the making of a new gallery.

The architect needed to resolve the contradiction at the heart of the conservation process described by Raphael Samuel in these terms: 'how far can 'adaptive re-use' be carried before it becomes something else?' Clearly the contradiction applies not only to conservation work, but to all work that claims to have an interest in the past and in the effects of time upon buildings.

Given the barely visible presence of the past, the contradiction is to a large degree unsolvable. To this extent, all new occupation is an infraction and it does violence to the past. Every conservation project, every conversion conceals effects that are analogous to the fire that once raged through 56 Artillery Lane. When Alex Sainsbury, the gallerist, purchased the property, the deed included the registered tenancy of Hannah and Rebecca Levy, two sisters who had lived in the building since the 1920s and who were then in their late 80s and mid 90s respectively.

Their parents, Jewish immigrants from Central Europe in the early 20th century, had been in service in the house, and their daughters had continued to live in an apartment in the attic. They did not marry and they had no children. The building had become vacant in the 1970s and they remained alone in the mostly vacant house.

Sainsbury offered them sheltered accommodation elsewhere, but they declined, replying that they were planning only one last move. The flat, its wallpaper, furnishings and appliances had not changed since the 1970s.

When building work started, workmen would occasionally fix things in it and the client assumed responsibility for their welfare. As 6a put it, 'you have some responsibilities when you are dealing with a grade 1-listed building, and you have others when you have tenants.' The point would not have been lost on Samuel. Hannah died in the course of the works, and Rebecca about a year after completion, at an age about a third of that of the building in which she spent all her life. Humans speak and buildings don't, buildings last (or some do) but humans don't. This causes confusion as to their respective significance and it raises doubts about the conventional presumption in favour of buildings. The more so as humans increasingly outlive buildings.

1970

2011

Much of the conversation between client and architect concerned the character of the space within which an artist might like to work and exhibit. Pursued beyond a certain point, neutrality becomes dull, cold and counterproductive. Thus, besides the management of the building history, there came a moment when the white world of the gallery space was introduced into the building from 'the other side', namely the client's, including new priorities that were unrelated to the existing context.

Until then, new parts had been shaped after old parts, for instance the charred timber panels and the cast iron handles and railings. All of a sudden old parts seemed to depend upon new parts. To simplify, construction, with all that it entails about building fabric and the ballast of the past, became overwhelmed by finishes.

A pair of pictures of Raven Row sums this up perfectly. A first image (already mentioned) shows a doorway ravaged by fire. The classical architectural details remain, stripped of their finishes and charred. The broken pediment above the doorway, the frieze of dentils above the architrave, the brackets running along the top of the wall, all are complemented by the equally fine but unintended details of cracks scorched into the timber surface by the flames. Smouldering mouldings, crackling dentils: the forces that opposed design intention and natural (or unintended) intervention appear equal, and the image is a powerful testimony to the strength and durability of human design. Only the thinner wood panels within the door completely disappeared, leaving gaping holes that seem so pure and immaterial in this tectonic inferno as to assume the unlikely appearance of mirrors.

A second image shows the same view of the gallery today. Black has turned into white, texture into sheen, dark into light, substance into air, timber into paint, and house into gallery. The space appears to have been bleached, as if it were not entirely here, here as well as there, ghostly, its pallor being consistent with the loss of human presence observed by 6a. Like an overexposed photographic print obtained from a more instantaneous and naturally darker negative. All told, the disparity within the pair of images is less a distinction between the old and the new of the kind that obsesses architecture historians than it is one between the living and the dead, the animate and the inanimate. It is less a question of heritage than it is one of natural history.

Making

The mind of architects is firmly trained on spatial narratives and images, but much of their lives is spent in the darkened spaces that precede them, surrounded by dust, cobwebs, droppings and debris. The discomfort of their situation is all in the caricature of the white-collared architect instructing blue-collared workers, the one in a spotless white shirt, the others in stained overalls.

Modernists, it is true, dreamt of factory-like building sites staffed by operators in white overalls. For all their efforts, between the fiction of design and the reality of the building site, in the no-man's land that separates architecture from building, there is to this day no logical path, no Ariadne's thread and very little comfort.

Between them, the gulf remains, socially, intellectually and practically, and it finds expression in 'detailing', an activity held in low esteem, commonly delegated to technicians who seek to bridge the gap between the flights of imagination of the architect and the turpitude of the building site. It is precisely here, in situations where fiction emerges with little or no mediation from the material, that 6a best like to operate. For this reason, the spontaneity of the fire that produced such a compelling and mysterious image (one that is 'more beautiful than anything that we could ever have made') burnt itself in their mind like a distant ideal.

A site is the result of a multitude of interventions. Some are well documented but most are part of the ebb and flow of life, of the whitening and darkening of things.

Together they form what Samuel described as *oldness*, a quality that owes as much to humans as to nature. What has been documented or listed is interesting, but not as interesting as the manner in which the original canvas became interwoven. Likewise, every project involves not only what the architect makes but all the things that were previously made. In making new things, in making them available for other people to use, the architect sets out or redirects an anthropological trajectory. All projects are anthropological because they are inscribed in a particular time and a particular place. 'All we do', say 6a, 'is set things off.'

The user, therefore, is not an abstract body, a statistical description that can be measured and moulded irrespective of its milieu, as in the digital architecture of the recent past. When one thinks about how to make things, one thinks, too, about how they shall be used. Some things are made for the hand, others, to walk on, and others still to look at. Humans use buildings in opportunistic ways. Likewise, 6a's details are opportunistic and seek to make the best of an occasion.

For instance the lower end of a handrail at Raven Row terminates with a small flourish, a slight whoosh that hyphenates the seeing eye with the grabbing hand. There is pleasure in the use of it. There is a pleasure, too, in the making of it, as several wooden variants made in the office prior to its casting in bronze aluminium testify.

In addition, other things defy prediction and remain unknown to the architect: 'the rest is out there, it's not me, it's not us, it's available.'

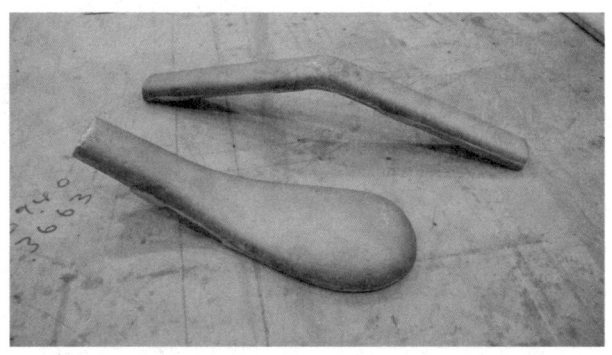

Neither anti-detail, as in Brutalism, nor virtuous craft, as in William Morris, 6a's details are free from ideology and morality. But they remain indebted to the idea that details communicate. For this reason, 6a are drawn to the photographic work of Richard Wentworth.

Some artists are interested in language. Others are interested in the making of things. But rarely, like Wentworth, are they interested in both. The way things are made can lead to a wider understanding of the city, of its culture and of its politics. 6a do not subscribe, however, to the view that architecture needs to make a statement. But they believe instead that architects make statements when they make things in a certain way as opposed to another.

'You make things for a particular reason: that is the statement.' But who really wants to know the reason, who wishes to observe and to interpret the statement? How often does the public scrutinize architecture in the same way they do works in an art gallery? Are the attitudes and the values that buildings make manifest necessary to the experience of architecture? Has not *ceci* – literature, the press – long ago killed *cela* – architecture's didactic capacity?

The two buildings where 6a have made their home once accommodated a printing works. One of these was weatherproof and housed the office. The other, following the departure of Pierre d'Avoine's office where Emerson had worked, became 'gardens of Babylon', overgrown and falling apart. Unsuited for computers, it accommodated (and still does in parts) a modest workshop including hand tools, benches, band saws and an extraction system. Used at first for model making, it became possible to build full-scale mock-ups in it, and in the space between the two buildings which a marquee covered almost exactly, large panels could be fabricated by two or three people.

6a eventually attracted staff with an appetite for making things, their preferred terrain being, as Germano Celant said of Arte Povera, where 'corporeality of material and gesture are brought into relation with our own bodies.'[5] Consider for instance the door handle designed for Raven Row. 6a looked at available handles but found them over-complicated. The prospect of designing a new one seemed more effort than it was worth. The client suggested using a previous design by 6a – an elongated knob cast in bronze aluminium – but wondered whether it was distinctive enough to suit Raven Row's character. In the course of the same meeting, Emerson pressed on one as if to create a divot and said: 'now it is.' Hence the present design with its thumb mark. 'The way of being is left to the use, to the material' (Celant again), the gesture being the intermediary between the one and the other.

In short, design was reduced to a gesture, the door knobs being like 6a's inadvertent signatures.

This anecdote is emblematic of 6a. It belies something concrete and personal, something manual that is present in the word 'manufacture'. On the one hand, the architect-as-detective is on the look-out for fingerprints – those of previous occupants. On the other, the architect-as-maker leaves his own fingerprints in the material, thus re-directing the experience of future occupants. If there were an ideal world of 6a, ideas would behave in it like gestures. They would have a corporeality and leave traces.

Tristan Tzara, Dada's foremost oracle, wrote that 'thought happens in the mouth.'[6] Poetry to him could never be spontaneous enough. One could say that, for 6a, 'thought happens in the hand.' This will seem less unreasonable, once it is remembered how well-placed is the hand, half-way between mind and material, with regard to the particular task of the architect. The hand – not the mouth, or the foot – is the human tool *par excellence* – and it is not difficult to imagine how strongly its presence must be felt by anyone genuinely interested in the making of things, in their manufacture.

Comedy

Architecture is a performance. More than the humour or the critique of modern architecture, it is this emphasis that 6a share with Jacques Tati, a one-time hero and occasional look-alike of Emerson (Wentworth, too, was influenced by Tati[7]). Tati's films are founded on the art of *reprise*, the short circus interlude performed by clowns during breaks between acts.[8] What distinguishes the *reprise*, like the parades that preceded the main performance in the traditional Italian theatre, is an impromptu, improvised quality.

It involves a re-enactment, in comic or tragic mode, of acts of skill and daring. It is an art of imitation that exaggerates and magnifies a situation and, in doing so, represents it with greater accuracy, as if through a looking glass.

Architecture of course does not represent situations, but it stages them. On rare occasions, it is itself a performance. One such occasion was the opening of *Hairywood*, the tower modelled by 6a after a set from *Les Vacances de Monsieur Hulot*. In its first setting at the Architecture Foundation in London, visitors queued at the foot of the tower to reach the cosy look-out.

Once at the top, they found themselves nose to nose, as it were, with passengers on the upper deck of passing double-decker buses. The situation was comical, but as in Tati's films it is not laughter that one remembers but an informality, a lightness of feeling, a kindness.

There is a human comedy engaging actions and situations. There is a comedy of things placed and misplaced by humans (Wentworth made it the subject of his photographs).[9] There is, too, a comedy of architecture that pits design intentions against materials and events. Guests form an orderly queue (of the kind once common at London bus stops) to access a tiny sitting room at the top of a tower. What appears to be a casting blemish becomes a spot for the thumb. The charred remains of a fire inspire the design of a façade.

Between the world of building and the world of inhabitation lies a fertile field for calculations and errors, for intentions and mishappenings. In this field lies a potential for expression that engages not the comedian, not the self-conscious expression of the Post-Modern architect but, as was the case with Tati, the staging of situations and the deployment of skills. In a sense, all architecture is a form of *reprise*, a temporary re-make, a fleeting make-believe.

A counterpart in the world of architecture to Tati's *reprise* is the building in which Tati lives in *Mon Oncle*. It includes courtyard, stair tower, connecting ramp, balcony and gazebo. The point of this construction is in the route taken by Tati to reach his home. Or rather there is to this construction not a point but a line that goes in and round, up and round again, down and out, forward and, after a full circle, into the gazebo that is Tati's home.

The line is a seemingly endless pirouette that is literally pointless – all that Tati does when he reaches his home is to adjust a window, re-directing the reflection of the sun onto a parakeet, causing it to launch into song. Little in the design of the set fits or is aligned. No two windows are alike.

One reveals Tati's upper body while another reveals his feet. Pleasure is the motive and fantasy is the rule. This building set is a work of bricolage. Its only composition is the curious arabesque traced by Tati's perambulation. Likewise, the concierge and the *petit monde* that has been gathered on the set represent a society that has no ulterior motive: a street sweeper who always stops short of sweeping, vendors who stop short of vending for they are always interrupted by conversation. Society itself is a work of bricolage, a never-ending comedy by which lives and things become entwined.

In *Mon Oncle*, the human comedy comes first, and the film set second, as a literal support to the action. The practice of architecture reverses this order. The designer creates spaces that, somehow, must be envisioned as inhabited by people. He must invest them with feelings – projecting his own in place of the occupants who do not yet exist. Hence the importance of techniques of representation to the architect.

Macdonald, herself an accomplished draftswoman, refers to Sempé who is to cartoons what Tati is to film. Sempé's drawings teem with life. In some street scenes, there are as many people as there are windows.

His industrious pen moves effortlessly from a fruit stall to the crowd milling around it. What is human and what is not are given the same weight. In the city described by Sempé, 'everything is inhabited', as Macdonald observes. Even when the street is empty, at night or in a snow fall, people remain the subject in their absence.

Sempé often sees in the city and in people a perceived grandeur and an absurdity. A man plays a large saxophone before a woman subdued in an armchair.

The scene is ridiculous but it is perceptive and gentle. It pricks at the same time as it enjoys the bubble. It reveals an intention of care comparable to Wentworth's photographs of human foibles and frailties along Caledonian Road. While still at college, Macdonald invited Wentworth to give a lecture at London Metropolitan University. Called 'The Cally and I' ('Cally' is for Caledonian Road, London), the talk lasted for two hours and left the audience 'skipping', feeling that people (not only what they make) are fantastic. In Wentworth like in Sempé, in Tati as well as in 6a, there is a fundamental optimism and a fascination with the resourcefulness of people as they get on with their lives.

In 'The Cally and I', Wentworth talked about people's details, not architects' details. It is not hard to imagine how refreshing and invigorating it might have been at the time. Young architects, though seduced by what Alison and Peter Smithson called the art of inhabitation, were immersed in the art of construction, in 'tectonics'. Theirs was primarily an architectural conversation, students in the studio of Caruso and St John for instance producing beautiful constructional essays (I simplify). For her part Macdonald, then in their teaching studio, presented her final project with a model that was like a doll's house.

Today still, 6a make doll's house-like models. Built at 1:20 scale, sometimes extremely detailed, they describe individual rooms to the extent that they can be inhabited with the eye – like Sempé's drawings. Architecture models describe buildings but dollhouses describe lived-in houses.

Bricolage

The magical world of the doll's house, the *making do and getting by* of Wentworth, the *reprises* of Tati do not belong with the careful planning of modernity. They appeal to a form of intelligence known to the Ancient Greeks as *metis*. There exists no treatise on *metis* comparable to those written on logic. *Metis* produced no philosophical system, no text that explains its fundamental characteristics and its origins.[10]

It is not even a concept. Its nature has never been made explicit and its procedures have not been justified. Yet it is clearly a form of intelligence, a way of thinking and of knowing that operates beneath the surface, being immersed in practical operations. *Metis* goes back and forth between the intelligible and the sensible, a quality that commends it to architects and to 6a in particular who can be said to practise it. Unlike engineering, it does not lend itself to precise measurement, to exact calculations and rigorous logic. It is instead an attitude that combines 'flair, wisdom, forethought, subtlety of mind, deception, resourcefulness, vigilance, opportunism, varied skills, and experience'.[11]

In pages that have since become famous, Lévi-Strauss made a similar distinction between the engineer and the *bricoleur*.[12] While the engineer works with materials and tools that have been procured and sometimes invented for the purpose of a particular project, the *bricoleur* works in a world that is closed and he makes do with what is at hand.

The set of materials and tools that he has at his disposal bears no relation to his project. Materials and tools are kept because they might come in handy. Whereas the trajectory followed by the engineer tends to be logical, the activity of the *bricoleur*, like the verb *bricoler*, describes an extraneous movement, a deviation. Thus Tati could be said to *bricoler* as he climbs from the *square* to his home in a series of turns and counter-turns.

The architect-*bricoleur* sniffs around, he rummages through old things, through materials and artifacts as well as ideas and concepts. He interrogates the heterogeneous objects that constitute his treasury, seeking to discover what each of them could signify. Like a detective, he looks for signs that might unlock a project (for instance the photograph of the burnt-out doorway at Raven Row) and he works round the restrictions imposed by the specific history of materials at his disposal.

The architect-*bricoleur* resembles the artist Giuseppe Penone who carves a timber beam in order to rediscover the tree within. He may find, like 6a, inspiration in Little Moreton Hall in Somerset, a medieval hall in which a multitude of timber elements can be traced back to a single tree.

Not for the first time have architects wanted to emulate the mentality of bricolage. Colin Rowe did so as a counter to Modernist planning in *Collage City*. Many architects saw in the sculptures of Picasso and in Cubism, for instance in the *papiers collés*, exemplars pointing away from the prissiness of much modern art.

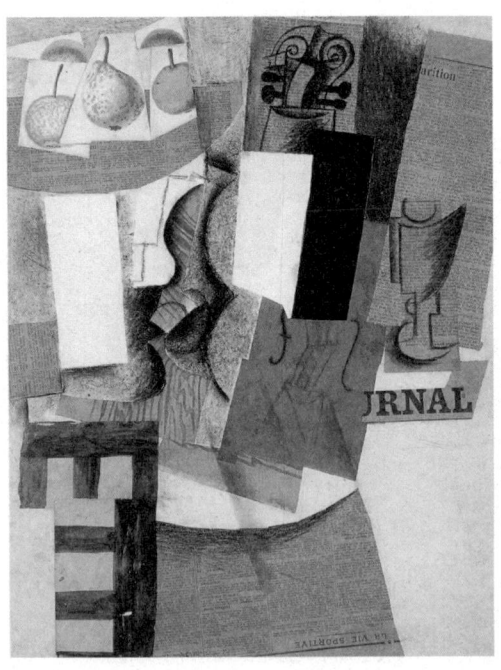

More generally, the study of non-western, 'primitive' societies by anthropologists, first among them Lévi-Strauss, became the basis for a critique of modern life. In 1972, Charles Jencks and Nathan Silver published *Adhocism: The Case for Improvisation*, an early attempt at interpreting the practice of bricolage for architects.[13]

In the wake of 1968, bricolage was imagined as a mode of direct action undercutting specialisation, bureaucracy and hierarchy. 'Instead of a city with ten thousand architects', Jencks argued, 'we need a city of ten million architects'. Everyone was to create his own personalised environment free from the 'idiocy and brainwashing' that were a legacy of Modernism – or so the authors rashly claimed. Adhocism called for small-scale activities that would permeate everyday life. It anticipated *The Language of Post-Modern Architecture* (only four years away) in its advocacy of pluralism and of a world 'built-up of fragments from the past'.

More relevant to 6a is Jencks' praise of Buster Keaton, of his fascination with gadgetry and his relentless ingenuity in finding new uses for old things. For Jencks, Keaton was a model of resourcefulness.

For 6a, Jacques Tati assumed this role and one is struck by the association, 30 years apart, of bricolage with two of the great figures of mime. 'Everything can always be something else', Jencks wrote in a short phrase that goes to the root of bricolage. A door knob is used to pull a tooth, a body becomes a canon ball, an inner tyre serves as a wreath in a funeral.

But what of expression? The Amazonian Indian assembles a mythology by using the debris of events that are part of the history of a society. The film actor finds in bricolage a source of humour. The artist deploys it to Surrealist or Dada-like effects. But what of the architect? For Jencks, adhocism elevated the botched solution into a subject for expression. His paragon was Bruce Goff, an architect who was not afraid to forego consistency. Nor was Robert Venturi who praised the 'honky-tonk displays' of the commercial urban scene. Arguably bricolage remained a key to the aesthetics of Postmodernism.

Writing a few years earlier than Venturi and Jencks, Lévi-Strauss' own vision of bricolage in art was indebted to *art brut*, and he offered as examples the *Ideal Palace* of the Facteur Cheval, the stage sets of Georges Méliès, and Mr. Wemmick's suburban 'castle' in Dickens' *Great Expectations*. Besides such raw, naïve aesthetic possibilities associated with popular art, Lévi-Strauss believed that bricolage could lead to brilliant insights on the intellectual plane, for instance in mythical thought.

For 6a, influenced as they were by Richard Wentworth, bricolage is a means to art, or to the part in architecture that is art. It is, too, an ethic: not that of the virtuous artisan but of the architect attentive to the nuances of human occupation and its effects on the fabric of buildings. Last, it is existential in that it revels in the comedy of making and unmaking that is a source of both pleasure and signification.

Bricolage also contributes its share of problems for architects. Its results are a compromise between means and ends – and architects are not known for their love of compromise. Bricolage invariably deviates from the initial project (which in any case was little more than a sketch). It can no more be reduced to a project (in the sense commonly understood by architects) than the *metis* of the ancient Greeks can be to a concept. Practically, it would presume that there be no contract between builder and client, or that the contingency clause of a contract be allowed to approximate the contract sum.

It is a low-tech equivalent of the computer-driven architecture of recent years that dreams of its own unfolding in real time. Not that 6a shun computers. On the contrary, computers are but one more tool added to the architectural set. In the dream world of real time architecture and spontaneous manufacture, whether at the work bench or at the computer keyboard, the project is constantly modified to absorb contingencies. It becomes dissolved in the process of its own making. Yet even Henri Bergson (the inevitable reference for an 'emergent' architecture) knew the difference between natural evolution and human work, between the spontaneous, open-ended emergence of life and the human plan that forecloses the future by drawing its form.[14]

Chance

Of course the architect-*bricoleur* starts with a plan, but unlike the architect-engineer of Modernism, his project is suffused with a sense of possibility and freedom. Sifting through the creations of the past and the debris of events, things address themselves to him as signs. Indeed everything around him is a sign, half-way between images and concepts. It is in this sense that Lévi-Strauss referred to bricolage as the 'science of the concrete'.

Through bricolage, the means and the ends of a project discover one another as it were by chance, according to the 'objective coincidence' theorised by André Breton in Nadja (and mentioned by Lévi-Strauss in *The Savage Mind*). For Breton, Nadja appears to be all sign, living in other times and other places. Yet she and Breton meet in a succession of unerring coincidences. Signs and facts collide with a mysterious evidence, like a plastic cup onto an iron spike or a woollen hat on a bollard in the photographs by Wentworth that testify to the improbable ways in which humans make do and get by.

Objective coincidence manifested itself at Raven Row in the chance discovery of archival photographs. Suddenly, the constrained regime of building conservation, the rank fastidiousness that seeks to reconstruct a hypothetical past caught fire in the minds of the architects, became less precious and more interesting.

The experiments that it later suggested, notably the casting of charred timber, eluded the spontaneity of the fire that inspired them in the first place. They belong to what might be called a subjective coincidence, of the kind Herzog & de Meuron and others made us accustomed to: decorative images and textures that are found, interpreted, replicated and stamped with the signature of the architect-author.

Objective coincidence must be sought elsewhere, for instance in what 6a describe as 'non-decisions'. At Raven Row, these came about as a result of the client's attitude to the works. While most clients wish to apply the effects of design evenly on the building fabric, Sainsbury preferred to concentrate interventions in certain areas and details, leaving other parts more or less as found. In the 18th century, the timber floors would have been covered with oil cloth or rugs. In the event, they were repaired by mixing and matching boards from various parts of the building and were neither sanded, varnished or covered.

The contrast with the walls and ceilings above is stark, as if rooms had been divided in two halves, one trodden, worn and sonorous, and the other whitewashed and silent. Elsewhere in the entrance, a concrete floor had been built at an earlier date for fire protection. It was never meant to be seen and was discovered in the course of the works beneath two layers of lino. A brief discussion ensued between client and architect, and so it remained, uncovered, rough and gritty to the foot.

Another non-decision is so evident as to have evaded the architects' attention. It arose from the agreement (clearly one that was not arrived at by design) not to press for the rehousing of the Levy sisters. Since their death, the apartment has remained unchanged. It now accomodates visiting artists, the furniture remains *in situ* where it was found.

This certainly is an instance of objective coincidence, bringing together old tenants with new owner in a kind of micro-history of Spitalfields. These non-decisions followed not a design intention but a simple question: should we just leave it? One later forgets that the exposed concrete and timber floors were barely intentional and they become no less integral to the character of the place than the parts upon which thought and effort were expended. Unlike the recent architecture inspired by Alison and Peter Smithson, they betray no obvious delight in the quality of things 'as found'. They are not set up as authentic relics or given aesthetic value. They are merely unfinished and they are allowed to collide, by an objective coincidence, with the more finished parts and with the art.

These non-decisions help to illuminate the meaning of bricolage. Through them, unpredictable events seem to overtake the will, the intentions and the authorship of the architects. For sure Keaton and Tati each have a distinctive style of acting, but it cannot be said of their jokes that they are typically Keaton's or Tati's. Rather they arise from the fortuitous collision between an artefact and a situation, a door handle and a toothache, an inner tyre and a funeral. For this reason, there can be no style, not even individual styles of bricolage.

The point was missed by Jencks and Silver who foresaw in adhocism 'the rebirth of a democratic mode and style'. Adhocism envisaged the decentralisation of design based on individual desire, a style appropriate to individualised consumption. Bricolage, by contrast, is a characteristic neither of individuals who personalise their surroundings, nor of the consumer goods that enhance their identities. It has no theory, no agenda, no preferred scale, no intellectual and formal tradition. But it leads instead to as many forms in the world of things as *metis* does in the world of thought.

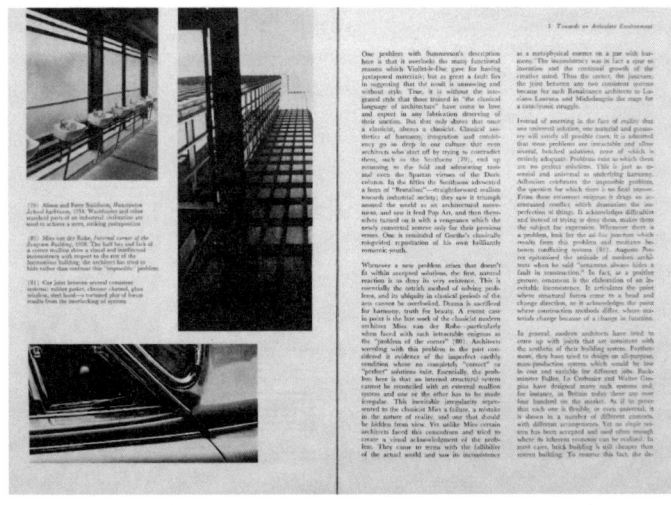

Anthropology

Raven Row is to 6a what the Lisson Gallery was to Tony Fretton. Both projects are seminal to their architects. Both needed an exegesis to make them accessible and recognisable to the public. In both, this exegesis took the form of photographs that prompted a particular way of seeing. Fretton at first declined to commission the conventional architectural pictures preferred by magazines. Instead he asked Chris Steele-Perkins of Magnum to take black-and-white, fly-on-the-wall photographs of the kind seen at news stands.

People were the subject. Fretton's point was clear: architecture must not be separated from everyday experience. Far from suppressing reflections on the glass (like architectural photographers do), Steele-Perkins emphasised them. He showed the building to be both modern in its transparency and 'critical' in its reflectivity – like the sculptures of Dan Graham that had been inspirational to Fretton and that were exhibited to celebrate the Lisson Gallery's opening.

In the case of Raven Row, the London Metropolitan Archive provided the photographs that have since become emblematic of the project. What they came to signify is less obvious, less self-conscious, more subtle than Steele-Perkins' photos for the Lisson. Some appear to document a valuable detail – a fireplace, a Rococo carving.

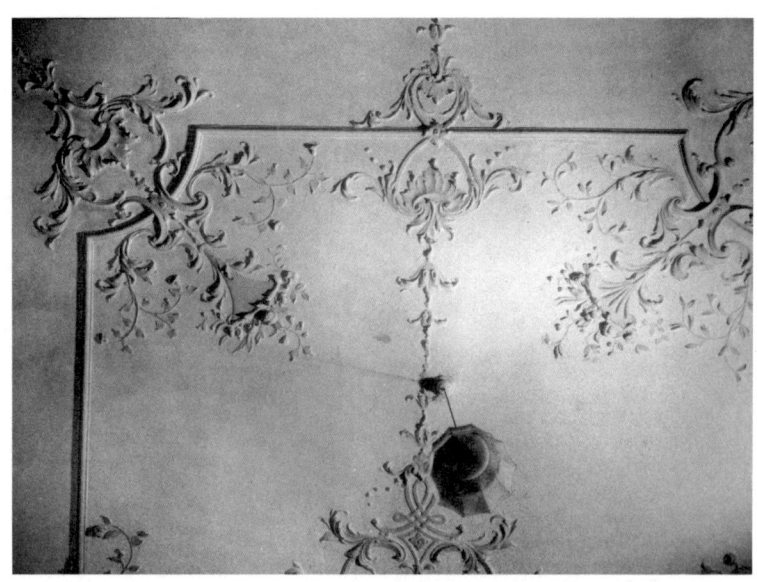

Another testifies to the fire. Yet another shows the modest furnishings of a bedroom in 1972. Unlike at the Lisson, there are no people in them and lives remain conjectural. Who took the photographs, in what year, and for what purpose: so much remains unknown. The 18th-century canvas remains visible, as do some of the stitches. But the lives have gone and the traces of occupancy are growing faint. As in the set of a *bricoleur*, events, traces of occupation are made available as signs for design. 6a repeated to me a phrase that I once said and had forgotten, namely that bricolage may be, quite simply, the making of things in the full and liberating awareness of how little we know. The pictures in the archive achieve precisely this: they liberate us in making us aware of how little we know.

Paradoxically, the human desertion caused by the passing of time makes us not less but more aware of the extent to which people and things are intertwined. 6a have the sensibility of anthropologists who combine in a single narration the sky, ancestors, the form of houses, the growing of yams, of manioc and rice, initiation rites, the forms of government and cosmogonies.[15] They likewise speak in the same breath of a devastating fire, the technical details of sash windows, the casting of bronze, Hannah and Rebecca Levy, the silk trade, room temperature, and the rituals of the art world.

There is not one process that applies to humans and another that applies to their environment, but a single process that unfolds in real time and governs their combined growth and development. There is not on the one hand a human ecology and on the other the environment, but a single ecology that encompasses the indivisible reality of the life process.[16] This helps in making sense of the discretion of the architecture at Raven Row, of its inconspicuousness as an object.

At Raven Row 6a found a guide in the design of 18th-century furniture. Prior to the invention of gas lamps, the ability to move a chair or a desk near a window or close to the fire was important. The proximity of light and heat were determinant.

Occasionally an entire activity was accommodated in a single piece of furniture. In a writing desk, for instance, paper, quills, ink, blotters were all assigned a specific place. Furniture was light, mobile and adjusted to situations. Hence, with the exception of the kitchen fittings that needed to be connected to plumbing and power, 6a made a rule that no furniture was to be fitted. As in Arte Povera, their form was to be obtained from the material and from the use. Tables, benches, cases were made as thin and as light as possible.

They remind me of what a Russian geographer called *corps meubles* or movable bodies, of the human predisposition for materials that have been dislodged from the surface of the Earth, for the rocks, gravel, sand, dust, vegetation, water, snow, air that can be moved and transformed with ease – like furniture.[17]

6a belong to the first generation of architects about whom it might be said that they have never been modern. For them, time is not a general framework that calls for the continuity of tradition, as it does with conservationists, or for the discontinuities of revolutions, as it did for Modernists. There is no element, as Bruno Latour argued, that does not evade the system, no object of which the date and the duration are not uncertain. Thus a people shall use both plastic buckets and goat skin bottles. Times have become mixed, like the photographs of Raven Row in the archive box, and 6a have developed a natural feeling for time and its vicissitudes.

The forms of the Moderns were pure and obeyed the *esprit de géométrie*. When hybrid, as in Le Corbusier's late works for the Capitole at Chandigarh, they were still composed with pure forms. For 6a, geometry remains important. But forms, however pure, however modern or classical, will in the end be sunken by the forces, human and non-human, that are arraigned against them. 'Most spaces', according to 6a, 'end up slouching from the ground up as well as fraying at the edges'. Form is a manifestation of the life-process itself, and there is no need for a distinct category of mind to account for it.[18]

What remains unclear is how this approach, this science of the concrete will cope with the increase in the size of commissions and the volume of work at 6a. Latour asserts that we have again all become pre-modern, yet he offers towards the end of his famous essay, *We have never been modern*, what seems like a concession and an afterthought. The greatness of the Moderns, he writes, comes from the proliferation of hybrids, from the extension of networks, from the acceleration in the production of traces. Their daring, their research, their innovation, their bricolage, their juvenile unreason, the ever greater scale of their action, this is, he exclaims, what we want to retain.

But can we, too, make without the Moderns' objectivity, without their coldness and their impersonality? What would become of 6a's personalised, concrete approach on a barren site, in the absence of an existing canvas, of a charismatic client, and of traces of previous lives and events? Modernism's love of science and of the laboratory, its admiration for engineering, its obsession with production and economies of scale, its cultivation of abstraction and repetition: none of this was gratuitous. Is it at all conceivable that the underlying causes survived, no doubt with some modifications, the disappearance of the attitudes that they once elicited?

Anthropology is commonly associated with the study of populations that are small in size and untouched by modernity, with the 500 Nambikwara of the Mato Grosso, the 4,500 Achuar on the frontier between Ecuador and Peru, the 800 Skolt Sámi in north-eastern Finland and adjacent Russia.[19] But Lévi-Strauss himself was far from indifferent to the New World. Indeed modernity offers rich pickings for anthropology. What, for instance, is *Delirious New York*, a eulogy of modernity like no other, if not an anthropological study of modern real estate and its attendant cosmology?

Besides, is engineering as averse to bricolage as Lévi-Strauss would have us believe? Consider for instance the Hubble telescope, this popular icon of modern science, clad with a light aluminium casing, fixed to a truss of graphite epoxy ('the same material used in many golf clubs, tennis rackets and bicycles'),[20] and wrapped in a blanket of insulation? How modern, this *soi-disant* high-tech marvel, this constant reminder of how little we know, that resembles nothing more than a tin can with an eye inside?

Irénée Scalbert

Notes ¹ The original four were Tom Emerson, Stephanie Macdonald, Alex Ely and Lee Marsden. ² The informal group included Tony Fretton, Mark Pimlott, Peter St John, Adam Caruso, Jonathan Sergison, Steven Bates, Jonathan Woolf, David Adjaye (for a time) and others. ³ 'Richard Wentworth in conversation with Tom Emerson', *AA Files*, no. 59, 2009 ⁴ Raphael Samuel, 'The Pathos of Conservation', in *The Saving of Spitalfield*, Douglas Balin et al. (eds), (London, 1989) ⁵ Germano Celant, *Arte Povera* (Milan, 1985) ⁶ Tristan Tzara, *L'Homme Approximatif* (Paris, 1930) ⁷ Marina Warner, *Richard Wentworth* (London, 1993) ⁸ David Bellos, *Jacques Tati: His Life and Art* (London, 1999) ⁹ *Richard Wentworth / Eugène Atget: Faux Amis*, with contributions by Peter Ackroyd. Geoff Dyer and Kate Bush (London, 2001) ¹⁰ Marcel Detienne and Jean-Pierre Vernant, *Cunning Intelligence in Greek Culture* (Paris, 1978) ¹¹ Ibid. ¹² Claude Lévi-Strauss, *Savage Mind* (London, 1966), chapter 1 ¹³ Charles Jencks first referred to bricolage in the article 'Adhocism on the South Bank', *The Architectural Review*, July 1968 [14] Henri Bergson, *Creative Evolution* (London, 1911), chapter 2 [15] See Bruno Latour, *We have never been modern* (London, 1993) [16] Tim Ingold, *The Perception of the Environment: Essays on Livelihood, Dwelling and Skill* (London, 2000), chapter 1 [17] Alexander Woeikof, 'De l'influence de l'Homme sur la Terre', *Annales de Géographie*, vol. x, 15 mars 1901 [18] Tim Ingold, *op. cit.* [19] These tribes were studied respectively by Lévi-Strauss, Philippe Descola (a friend of Bruno Latour), and Tim Ingold. [20] www.hubblesite.org

Captions ᵖ·⁰⁵ New gallery at Raven Row, London, by 6a architects (2009). Photo David Grandorge ᵖ·⁰⁸ *Patio and Pavilion* installation for *This is Tomorrow*, Whitechapel Gallery, London (1956) by Eduardo Paolozzi, Alison & Peter Smithson and Nigel Henderson. Photo Nigel Henderson Estate ᵖ·⁰⁹ Model of Alison & Peter Smithson's Arts Barn at the University of Bath (1980–81). Built for the exhibition *Two Kinds of Wild* by Diploma Unit Two (Peter Beard and Tom Emerson) at the Architectural Association, London (2003). Photo Sue Barr ᵖ·¹¹ Exterior paving at the New Art Gallery Walsall by Caruso St. John & Richard Wentworth (2000). Photo Hélène Binet ᵖ·¹³ Raven Row seen from Frying Pan Alley, by 6a architects (2009). Photo 6a architects ᵖ·¹³ The Lisson Gallery (designed by Tony Fretton). Interior as seen from the street (1991). Photo Chris Steele-Perkins/Magnum Photos ᵖᵖ·¹⁴⁻¹⁵ New gallery at Raven Row by 6a architects showing *The Stuff That Matters*. Textiles collected by Seth Siegelaub for the CSROT (2012). Photo 6a architects ᵖ·¹⁶ Raven Row seen from Frying Pan Alley, by 6a architects (2009). Photo David Grandorge   p.18 New Art Gallery Walsall by Caruso St. John (2000). Photo Hélène Binet   p.19 Garden Room, South London Gallery, by 6a architects (2010). Photo 6a architects   p.20 Model of Garden Room, South London Gallery, by 6a architects (2010). Photo 6a architects   p.21 Interior, Clore Education Studio, South London Gallery, London, by 6a architects (2010). Photo David Grandorge   p.22 Clore Education Studio, South London Gallery, by 6a architects (2010). Artwork Dan Perjovschi, *I put a spill on you*, 2010, wall drawing, permanent marker. Courtesy of the artist; Gregor Podner Gallery, Berlin; and Lombard-Freid Projects, New York. Photo 6a architects   p.23 Clore Education Studio, South London Gallery, by 6a architects (2010). Photo 6a architects   pp.24–25 Clore Education Studio, South London Gallery, London, by 6a architects (2010). Photo David Grandorge   p.26 New gallery, South London Gallery, by 6a architects (2010). Artwork, Ernst Caramelle, *Untitled*, 2010.

Photo 6a architects   p.31 Archive photograph of interior at 58 Artillery Lane, June 1914. The interior was moved to the Chicago Art Institute in the 1920's and returned to the building in 2008. Photo courtesy City of London Metropolitan Archives   p.35 Archive photograph of No. 56 Artillery Lane, 1971. Photo courtesy City of London Metropolitan Archives   p.37 Detail of fire damage in Front Room at No. 56 Artillery Lane. Photo courtesy City of London Metropolitan Archive   p.39 Yaki-sugi-ita, Takeshi Hayatsu of 6a architects directing charring of cedar cladding for Raven Row (2008). Photo 6a architects   pp.40–41 Charred cedar roof cladding at Raven Row. Photo 6a architects   p.44 First floor front room of No. 58 Artillery lane awaiting reinstallation. Photo 6a architects   p.47 Hannah and Rebecca Levy apartment, fourth floor, 56–58 Artillery Lane, built in 1972. Photo David Grandorge (2010)   p.51 Interior, second floor, 56 Artillery Lane (1971). Photo courtesy City of London Metropolitan Archives   p.51 Interior, fourth floor, 56–58 Artillery Lane, built in 1972.

Photo David Grandorge (2010)   p.53 Ground floor gallery, Raven Row, by 6a architects. iPhone photo 6a architects   p.55 Fire damage in Front Room at No. 56 Artillery Lane. Photo courtesy City of London Metropolitan Archive (1972)   p.57 Refurbished interior, 56 Artillery Lane (2009). Photo David Grandorge   p.60 South London Gallery during construction (2009). Photo 6a architects   pp.64–65 Archive photograph of first floor interior, 58 Artillery Lane (1971). Photo courtesy City of London Metropolitan Archives   p.68 Raven Row cast handrail, by 6a architects (2009). Photo 6a architects   p.69 Raven Row cast handrail pieces, by 6a architects (2008). Photo 6a architects   pp.70–71 New gallery at Raven Row, Artillery Lane, London, by 6a architects (2009) Photo David Grandorge   p.72 *Making Do & Getting By*, Regent's Park, London, Early C21st, Richard Wentworth.   p.74 Workshop, 6a architects (2007). Photo 6a architects   p.77 Sand cast doorknob, Raven Row, London, by 6a architects (2009). Photo 6a architects   p.84 Martine (played by Nathalie Pascaud) at her window during the filming of *Les Vacances de M. Hulot* by Jacques Tati (1953) André Dino / Les Films de Mon Oncle   p.85 Manon at her window. Hairywood by 6a architects with Eley Kishimoto (2005). Photo David Grandorge   pp.86–87 Hairywood rebuilt in Covent Garden, London, for Skin & Bones: Parallel Practices in Fashion and Architecture, Somerset House, 2008, by 6a architects with Eley Kishimoto (2008). Photo David Grandorge   p.91 The house of M. Hulot from *Mon Oncle* by Jacques Tati (1958) Les Films de Mon Oncle   pp.92–93 Extension, South London Gallery, London, by 6a architects (2010). Photo David Grandorge   p.97 Illustration by Jean-Jacques Sempé, from *Un Peu de Paris* (2001). Jean-Jacques Sempé / Éditions Gallimard.   p.98 Illustration by Jean-Jacques Sempé, from *Les Musiciens* (1979). Jean-Jacques Sempé / Éditions Denöel (1979, 1996)   p.101 Model, Romney House, by 6a architects (2012). Photo 6a architects   p.103 Romney House, London, by 6a architects (2012). Photo 6a architects   p.111 Giuseppe Penone working on *Cedro di Versailles*, 2000.

Photo Archivio Penone   p.112 *Still Life with Violin and Fruit (winter 1912)* Pablo Picasso, Succession Picasso / DACS, London 2012.   p.115 Buster Keaton pulling tooth using a door in *The Scarecrow* (1920). Image courtesy of Cohen Film Collection LLC   p.116 Raven Row, London, by 6a architects (2009). Photo David Grandorge   p.118 Buster Keaton sliding down a balustrade in *Neighbors* (1920). Image courtesy of Cohen Film Collection LLC   p.121 South London Gallery, by 6a architects (2010). Artwork by Gary Woodley, *Impingment No. 56*, 2010, PVC. Courtesy of the artist. Photo 6a architects   p.122 Romney House, London, by 6a architects (2012). Photo 6a architects   p.123 Romney House, London, by 6a architects (2012). Photo 6a architects   p.130 *Making Do & Getting By*, Walworth, London, Early C21st, Richard Wentworth.   p.133 Charred cedar roof cladding at Raven Row. Photo 6a architects   p.134 Cast iron façade with vents, Raven Row, London, by 6a architects (2009). Photo David Grandorge   p.137 Ground Floor, Raven Row, London, by 6a architects (2009). Photo David Grandorge p.141 Pages 76–77 from *Adhocism: The Case for Improvisation* (1973) by Charles Jencks & Nathan Silver, showing (clockwise from top left) *Hunstanton School bathroom*, by Alison and Peter Smithson (1954), *Internal Corner of the Seagram Building*, by Mies van der Rohe (1958) and *Car Joint Between Several Consistent Systems*, photo by Charles Jencks (1973)   p.144 The Lisson Gallery (designed by Tony Fretton) as seen from the nearby schoolyard (1991). Photo Chris Steele-Perkins / Magnum Photos   p.146 Carved plaster ceiling with lamp, No. 58 Artillery Lane, June 1953. Photo courtesy City of London Metropolitan Archives   p.150 Second Floor, Raven Row with *La Lingère* shelves by 6a architects, as shown in *The Stuff That Matters. Textiles collected by Seth Siegelaub for the CSROT* (2012). Photo 6a architects   p.151 Shelf detail of La Lingère shelves by 6a architects (2010). Photo 6a architects   pp.152–153 Display tables by 6a architects in main gallery during *The Stuff That Matters.* Textiles collected by Seth Siegelaub for the CSROT, Raven Row, London (2012). Photo 6a architects

Never Modern 03
Situation 29
Intervention 43
Making 59
Comedy 81
Bricolage 105
Chance 129
Anthropology 143

Notes 162
Captions 164

Irénée Scalbert is an architecture critic and historian. He studied at the Architectural Association, London, in the late 1970s and joined its teaching staff in 1979, holding various responsibilities including Master in History and Theory. He is best known as a historian for his essays on Alison and Peter Smithson and James Stirling. A long-standing interest in housing led to the publication of his book on Jean Renaudie, *A Right to Difference*. He has written many critical essays on contemporary architecture, notably on Caruso St John and FOA. On several occasions, he has been Visiting Professor at the Graduate School of Design, Harvard University. He currently teaches at SAUL in Ireland and he lives in London.

Never Modern
by Irénée Scalbert and 6a architects

Special thanks to Pamela Johnston from the AA Print Studio for reviewing and editing the text.

Published by Park Books
Niederdorfstrasse 54
8001 Zürich – Switzerland
www.park-books.com

Designed by John Morgan studio

Typeset in Starling

© 2013 text: Irénée Scalbert
© 2013 6a architects, London, and Park Books, Zürich

Printed in Belgium by die Keure

ISBN 978-3-906027-24-1